Dear Elizabeth

by

Mary E. Lally

Printed in Victoria, Canada

Note for Librarians: a cataloguing record for this book that includes
Dewey Classification and US Library of Congress numbers is available
from the National Library of Canada. The complete cataloguing record
can be obtained from the National Library's online database at:
www.nlc-bnc.ca/amicus/index-e.html
ISBN 1-4120-2218-5

TRAFFORD

This book was published   on-demand in cooperation with Trafford Publishing.
On-demand publishing is a unique process and service of making a book available for
retail sale to the public taking advantage of on-demand manufacturing and Internet
marketing. On-demand publishing   includes promotions, retail sales, manufacturing,
order fulfilment, accounting and collecting royalties on behalf of the author.

Suite 6E, 2333 Government St., Victoria, B.C. V8T 4P4, CANADA

Phone	250-383-6864	Toll-free	1-888-232-4444 (Canada & US)
Fax	250-383-6804	E-mail	sales@trafford.com
Web site	www.trafford.com	TRAFFORD PUBLISHING IS A DIVISION OF TRAFFORD

HOLDINGS LTD.
Trafford Catalogue #04-0046   www.trafford.com/robots/04-0046.html

10   9   8   7   6   5   4   3   2

"We can not do great things ~ only small things with great love"
Mother Theresa

Mary Lally has written a beautiful tribute to her mother in "Dear Elizabeth". Many of us will experience the death of a loved one but it takes a very rare individual to be able to put that period of time into words. "Dear Elizabeth" will touch not only your heart but down to the center of your soul. Mary has managed to do something that very few of us will be ever capable of. She opens up her heart and her life to share with you the experience in losing her mother to cancer. Their story is a rare look into the last few months that two extraordinary women were able to share. It is full of love but more importantly, full of laughter, right up until the end of their journey together here on earth. "Dear Elizabeth" is a love letter, one of the purest in nature. It is a gift to her mother, the woman that raised her and loved her the only way she knew how. Many of us have run away from such an experience to shield our hearts from the feelings that one goes through when losing someone you love. Mary teaches us that the greatest gift you can give someone is just to be there, holding them tightly, right until their last breath. It is the only real glimpse we get into the gates of heaven.

Elizabeth gave Mary the gift of life, and in turn, Mary gave Elizabeth the gift of unconditional love in death.

In Love,
Mary Sierra

Acknowledgments

This correspondence of sorts is dedicated to Elizabeth for obvious reasons, then too I would like to dedicate it to the people in my life who stayed in spite of me. For Lorrie who freed me from myself, to Judy who had a dream and lives it. To Anita, who never left me by the way side and to Barbara who keeps me from falling by the way side. Many thoughts to Diane who can win an argument without saying a word. Without her guidance I'd still be arguing and lost. To the Porter's of Northport who never threw a stone, and to gra who taught me how to give. To Agnes, where ever she may be. To Camille and Marian who were always near by from the beginning. To my sister Helen and my brother Sean, the two who stayed.

To my sister-in-law Terry, who "rose to the occasion" towering in strength, when others cowered in grief. To my brother Mike and his wife Kathy, who in spite of family feud were always there when the chips were down. To Mary and Elma who where there for me without question, holding my broken heart with their silent, peaceful presence. That moment will live within me through eternity. To Mike Simon, who believed in me with laughter and without judgment. To Dr. Winter and Dr. Radansky who saved my life. And to those of you who have selected to read **Dear Elizabeth**, *I hope that somewhere in the words I have chosen to write that you have found some small piece of solace. If you have, please, pass it on to others, so that they too might know that we are never really left alone in our time of what seems to be insurmountable darkness. Those whom we have loved who have moved on to greater triumphs are only but a whisper away. All you have to do is listen to know they are there....*

For Connie & Jim Mckillop
And
Jamie, Christen, Sean, David, Colin, Paula,
Kathleen, Peter, Meg, Kelly, Vito, Regina & Brian

may the road rise up to
meet you,
may the wind be always at
your back
may the sun shine warm
upon you face,
the rains fall soft upon
your fields and,
until we meet again, may
God hold you in
the Palm of His hand... ...

I

Dear Elizabeth,

I am writing Elizabeth and not mom with great caution. You can kill me for calling you that. I mean no disrespect to you, quite the contrary. It is Christmas Day; some one hundred thirty odd days have passed since you went away. It seems like yesterday. This day like many others, are "firsts" in my life. They are not easy, I am uneasy and clumsy and I miss you terribly. So I thought I'd write to you. No, I don't have a job yet but I will get one. I spend my days busy trying to keep busy.

When you first left, there was no time to mourn. There was no quiet, no peace. I don't

5

know what you were thinking when you chose who you chose to execute your will. Your choice was in poor judgment. I'm sorry mom, but if you were here, you'd kill him. His judgment borders on the ridiculous, somewhat of a joke. Considering that all you had of any value was your house, your children and grandchildren. I call him the executioner of the will. It appears he is just that, an executioner. In one fell swoop; he was able to destroy what little hope there was that this family could become a family once again. Tears were from aggravation and hurt, not sadness about your leaving. It angered me tremendously that I could not mourn you. That I couldn't just lay in peace and cry for myself and the loss of you. I am able to do that now, and you're not even here to say, "Stop crying or I'll give you something to cry about"... I know how you hated talking about things. So in order to keep some things the same, I'll do the talking, and in order to show you just how much things have changed since you left, I will not skirt the truth. Now that I know how truly brave you are, I will not be afraid about how I think the truth will hurt you. I learned a lifetime of you in less than a year's time. What a wonderful gift from God. I would like to share that, if that's okay. Don't worry, I won't tell them everything...

My life changed dramatically when you went away. Nothing looks, feels or happens the way it all used too. Days sometime seem to go on forever. In my forever days, I think back about all that went on before you had to leave. Ma, there was so much. Now that you and dad are both gone, it seems insurmountable. With both of you gone, there is no one to tend the children. There is no hierarchy, no one to answer to, and no one to make peace. Havoc, hate and the ridiculous, have emerged. Every grudge held from childhood through adulthood has made an appearance. It started immediately. It destroyed the mourning process, and has left a bitter taste. But it happens everywhere, from Park Avenue to Smith Street. Our family is not unique in that way mom. You gave one person a tad of power, and he took it and ran with it. And he can keep running with it for all it is worth. I believe there will be a final judgment for all of us. I pity him.

Aside from that tacky subject, life goes on without you, ever so slowly. I am so very grateful for having spent the last days of your life with you. I learned from you and I know you learned from me, not that you would ever tell me that. But I know, because every night when I put you to bed, you thanked me for being there. You the mother of eight children, allowed me to get you ready for bed and tuck you in. Of course when I came back to check on you, you would laugh and I couldn't help it. I knew you were so very sick and you were putting up such a front, I had to come back and check on you each and every night. I used to panic after I put you to bed thinking, what would I do if you left sometime in the night and I found you in the morning. I was scared to death. I remember sitting in the kitchen, with my coffee in the morning straining to hear some kind of noise from the upstairs, so I knew it would be safe to go up. Your daily rituals from being okay to being sick changed drastically and at the end, quickly. You had no set ways anymore. The sicker you became, the less reliable your routine was. It seemed okay for us not to have a set routine. As long as your coffee was all right, I was not in trouble. I believe we went by the seat of our pants, something we both somehow did to make that time less painful. I think we did it rather well together.

The first time you got sick, was the worst. For almost that entire year that you refused to see a doctor, dad and all eight of us talked about how you were every other day. It was sad and frustrating to listen to you not going out somewhere or going out somewhere and getting sick. How did you do it? What happened that

9

turned you so against doctors? You went almost a whole year losing weight, spending more time in the bathroom than hours slept in a night. You were really hurting. Nothing anyone said made any difference, you'd be all right, you knew better. At the same time, you knew deep in your heart that there was something very wrong with your body. You were petrified to know, as would anyone. So you kept your mouth shut but we still knew. I am sure in this "I know something you don't know", "I think", family, someone must know what happened to you to make you finally give in and find a doctor.

I remember your reaction to the word cancer. You raised your hands to your head saying "no", "no" shaking your head back and forth. Dad never budged but he did stop for your Starbucks coffee on the way home. The poor guy, he was really shook mom. It seemed things happened so quick after that. Doctors, hospital surgery, doctors home, chemo radiation, and

you're learning to live your life differently now.
You hated that colostomy; from the day you got it
to the day you died. However, it saved your life.
It's very possible that you being so stubborn
played a part in the end result, which is sad. It
may have been different otherwise, who knows.
One thing about your stubbornness though, it
saved your life the second time around, there's no
doubt in my mind. You were a winner when you
left. I wish that you could see that and believe it.
Your life at least, what I know of it, was no picnic.
You had smarts, looks but no father. You had a
roof over your head but no one to come home to.
A single mother was raising a single child, her
young husband taken from her without warning.
How could she have been there for you? There
was no one there for her when she was a child. An
alcoholic mother left Gra, her sister, and her
brothers in an orphanage. Gra couldn't help it
mom, she didn't know she had to be there for you.
She thought you were rough and tough, as she

had to be. Grama was before her time, she was a pioneer in the world of single working mothers. One of the best nurses I have ever known. Unfortunately, she was never the mother you wanted, just as you couldn't be the mother I wanted. Gra was there for you all through your life in ways that she could be. Just as you were for me in the ways you could be. It changed for you and Gra later in the years, just as the last couple of years and that last year of your life had changed for us. I am so grateful to you. I know how hard things were for you. I will never forget the expression on your face when you said, " I wish grama was here so I could put my head on her shoulder", You were becoming frightened. I was so happy to hear you say that about grama, but uncertain of what to do about your fear. I couldn't let you know that I knew of your fear. You would have thrown me out "on me rear" if I dared insinuate that you were afraid of something. So many times I found myself wishing daddy could have been there. Not sick as he was, but just there. That whole time was a nightmare. It was scary that you were just getting done with treatment for a deadly disease to stay alive, and he was slowly giving up on life. How it must have felt, barely back on your feet and he got sick. In his own way, he tried very hard to die. He was a tired man. You couldn't ask more of a man as far a providing for a family like he did. He didn't have time for much else. Two, sometime three jobs at once left us little time with him. When he was home, he was sleeping or trying to. I often wonder what I was thinking when I put my marbles in his mouth when he was sleeping. I wonder too what dad was thinking when according to your number one son; dad beat him up.

I am sorry for you, that the last five or so years of your life you were so filled with craziness. So many times I thought to myself that it wasn't supposed to be like this. You and dad were supposed to do all the things you wanted to do.

You and dad had the money, had the time, but you didn't have the energy. When he stopped going fishing, it was all down hill. He was never the same. The man whom I had grown up with, had gone somewhere far, far away.

I never really understood people taking care of people who had the craziest of relationships, until I came to care for you. I know of so many couples and have heard so many mind-boggling stories about spouses who wanted to kill each other for fifty years. Suddenly showing what love is all about when one or the other took ill. Sure, they still had their moments but they were still there, tending not only to a spouse but also to all the other things that come along in twilight years. I watched you with dad, and sure, you still wanted to kill him most of the time but you didn't put him out on the street. I know you were angry with him when he was sick, at the same time you were sick. You were angry with him for leaving you when the cancer came back the second time.

When we talked about him later on in your illness,
I was never sure if you hated him for things he did
or hated yourself for never doing whatever it was
you wanted to do instead of having eight kids.
What would you have done mom. Gone to
Hollywood and had Tyrone Powell kiss you on
the beach, or married a millionaire, had a boy and
a girl and lived on the "Gold Coast". Would you
have married a lighthouse keeper and tended to
the light. You always talked about how the
pioneer women made it across the country and
how heroic they were. Nothing mom is more
heroic than having eight kids, surviving
alcoholism and fighting death with every breath
you took.

I am not sure having dad around when you
got sick would have helped things. Dad was
never good when someone was sick. He was great
in an emergency, but if your illness lingered, he
became sicker than all hell. So, you got better
quickly. It was better that way. No competition for

the couch. You always said when you were pregnant dad used to get sick. The more things change, the more they stay the same. You got cancer, and he died.

Fifty-six years, no warranties, no guarantees. Something was always broken, be it a child or an appliance. Adopted pets lasted long enough to die or headed for greener pastures after a short stay. Adopted people at our house did the same as pets. There was always a stray at the dinner table. In addition, it was not unusual for the couch to be a part time bed. What were you thinking all that time? Some of our "adoptees" stayed a long time. After a while things just blended into things, people blended into people. When you ran out of forks, the table was set. Spoons were a commodity, best use for them were diggin' mud in the "backayard". You were always yelling about the silverware disappearing. Someone said at your funeral that you were very proud we never had eggs for dinner. Are you sure about that? Sorry, you're right, we never had eggs for dinner. We had spaghetti for breakfast, but never eggs for dinner. Life is great isn't it? The seating arrangement at that dining room table stayed the same, up until number one and number two sons became property of the United States Government. Even when daddy wasn't there, it stayed the same except for the one who wanted to sit in daddy's seat. This always caused a fight, which in the end left daddy's seat empty anyway.

Time came along and changed everything and everyone. Some of the broken branches of my life were not supposed to happen the way they happened. The death of dad, and the way he died were never a thought in my mind. Neither yours. I never thought about it I guess. I knew we would all die someday but I never tried real hard to think about it. I actually thought you were going to die at a much younger age but I never thought about how you would die. Who knows any way? Before test tubes, we were pretty much all born the same way, we just never know how or when we are going die. I think its God's way of keeping us on our toes. You know mom, In my heart I truly believe that when you are told you have a terminal illness and only have a certain amount of time left here as a mortal, you are given a gift. You can make real plans. Not maybes, what ifs, or we'll see. You are forced to live life as we should all live it everyday, with every ounce of life we can muster. When you lay in bed at night you will thank God with all your heart for the day just done and when you rise in the morning, thank Him for another sunrise. I heard you mom, in the night and in the morning. You convinced me. I think too that you go through all the "stages" of a dying person. You make plans, say things you would ordinarily leave to another time, you do things and look more intently at what you're doing. When you think no ones listening, you reminisce about days gone by. You finally realize what life is all about. Damn all those "live for the day" slogans, they were right mom. Towards the end mom, when you could, you lived for the moment. I watched you, as your time dwindled down, you were becoming a very different person. You talked about God often; you talked about life more earnestly than I had ever heard you do. You and I laughed with each other, at each other and for each other. It was the best.

The gift of knowing you were going to die sooner than expected, I think gave you the chance to become the person you were never able to be and not to give a damn what others thought. Afraid, reminiscent, funny, sad, and much closer to people than you had ever been before. I know how difficult that was for you. You were tough stuff mom. I don't think you hurt people intentionally; I think it came from all your sadness. Your era of people were stifled. It could have been an "Irish thing" or it could be because of the "church", whatever your reasons for sticking it out, you did. You bore and raised eight kids and influenced countless of others. Through the fifties, sixties and seventies, you came up against an enormous amount of rhetoric. From me running away all the time to someone else doing what kids did the best back then: driving the nuns to call every day. Your punishments were pretty tough. Probably not allowed in this day and age. Your wooden spoon approach was the one that will remain with me. When you could catch us, hair pulling was up there but it was nowhere near as artful as when the nuns did it. I know I have the record for times runaway.

I made an art of it. I must have been a glutton for punishment. I ran away because of a beating and then got beat for running away. Some twenty years after my escapades, you met a Police officer who often brought me back. He asked if I was still running away, you said "no", "She just moves around a lot". I still have the urge to go. Though I must be getting old, before I go anywhere now, I try to plan on getting where I'm going, and getting back, without the police. My sense of adventure is dimming.

Now that I'm thinking about it, all eight of us kids were "known" for something. One for building one single car from parts of four or five other cars that lined the driveway. That one single car will always stay with me. The driver's door did not open one day and you and a bee met up in the front seat. I don't know what scared us in the back seat more, you screaming or the bee that was much more scared than we were. You really, never had a new car until 1972. Before that it was always purely guesswork as to whether you had a running car. I remember when we got our first "automatic". It was a Chevy, and three of us and you left the driveway in reverse okay. It was when you tried to go forward that the trouble started. You would mistake the brake for the clutch, attempting to change gears. We would stop short, very short. The three of us in the back seat were repeatedly thrown to the floor. At the first stop sign, we got out. You yelled and we stood there on the curb peeing ourselves. We walked home and you went on bucking down the road.

You drove your beautiful new car until the end. We were always worried that you shouldn't have been driving but you wouldn't hear of it. You were rowing your own boat. I knew when I was coming to shop for you that you were waning from your driving. You gave it up gracefully. You never said you weren't going to drive anymore, you just became too tired and weak. When you let me drive your beautiful car, I knew you were giving in to another part of your demise. You never gave up anything without a fight. Even going up all those stairs, every night to your bed, no matter how long it took, you fought all the way. No one but me knew that you didn't even have the strength to stand and make the coffee any more. When I started coming to see you for more days than not and some questioned my being there telling me to mind my own business, you saw my hurt and promptly told me to tell them where to go. I should have told them but I never did. Your stubbornness used to drive me nuts but in the end, it was what kept you going and what gave you the peace you had when you died. I will always admire that and I will never forget it. You knew what you were doing all along.

And not only that, for the first time in your bloody life, people were agreeing with what you were doing. They all believed you were doing the right thing. You, a mother in modern times doing the right thing. I'll be damned. Just kidding. They encouraged you as best they could. But you know there was always that fear factor covering everything. Your fear of dying and our fear of you dying. A lot of times you weren't sure if people were really behind you or just saying they were. I know there were times when you yourself were uncertain if you were doing the right thing. But you stood your ground, pushed, pulled and cried and just kept right on going. There were some days when I could see your fear. If you think you were scared, you should have been in my sneakers. I wanted you to protect me, and be the mommy. Sometimes I could soothe you in ways you could accept and sometimes no matter what I said, it was wrong. You hated "mushy". I had to teach myself ways to let you know it was okay to be scared without being "mushy". And damn most of the time didn't I blow it. But I got better at recovery. I could cover up my mushy real quickly towards the end. Either that or you were just too damn sick to bother getting uncomfortable. Everyday I learned something about you. And everyday you and I laughed about something. No matter how you pained and how I feared somehow you and I had a good laugh, everyday. Nobody knows that but you and me. Should I tell them? I know I promised you I wouldn't tell them everything, and I won't. I wouldn't do that to you. The family continues to play secrets. The ones with the biggest secrets have the biggest mouths to speak the least sense with. What good would it do to tell them we laughed everyday. They wondered why I was there at all. Hold on for this one mom, I sometimes find myself feeling sorry for some of them. Not all of them. Just some of them. Eight people, eight stories. All from the same family and they all saw their childhoods differently. Some forgave, some didn't know how to, some just wouldn't and the ones who did, were able to leave the past behind. Those who stayed in the past are still there.

I went to your house today. I sat in the car in the driveway. The house seems to stand there in such silence. Man, mom, so much happened inside the walls of that house. For ten people, it's not a very big house. Two real bedrooms, a converted attic and hallway, for more sleepers. One and a half baths. I say one and a half baths because there was never a time, when everything worked in both bathrooms at the same time at any given time. But we made out okay didn't we? You grew up in that house, more than once. It truly was YOUR house. You know mom that was the only thing I ever heard you say was yours with any conviction; "It's my house". It still is. Your house will live on and on in so many peoples lives. All those who managed three squares and a cot when you were growing up added to those rascals who we brought home now and then adds up to quite a register of guests. Every one of those people is part of, and has a story to tell of your house. Your house has seen so many changes in the neighborhood. It watched when they elevated the railroad tracks. It stood when they razed the wooden firehouse and built the present one in 1955. Houses to the east of it are long gone. To the west are concrete monsters that took away the view of your incredible sunsets. No matter, you stayed. You tried like hell to have a decent looking house. You never wanted "shanty Irish" for your house. No matter how hard daddy tried to keep it "shanty Irish", you just kept at him. You were determined to have your house stand tall and pretty. You had your white picket fence, (done while daddy was in the hospital) and dad had his flagpole. Your house may be silent, but it stands tall and pretty. They were coming to do something to the house today, so I couldn't stay long. I wanted to get in somehow, but there is no way. I will probably never feel or see the inside of your house again in my mortal life. The executioner changed the locks, shortly after you left. I don't know why he had to do that. The only two people who had keys, were Sean and I. There was really nothing to be locked out from except memories. How that breaks my heart. Some of them just don't get it, do they mom. I saw the reflection of my tears in the car window. I had to leave. I miss your house mom. I miss you. All the years we spent fighting each other were worth it in the end. We learned of each other in a very special way. Perhaps because we no longer had wooden spoons and working legs. I had with you in seven or eight months what we missed in a lifetime. Life is good!

It wasn't easy for either of us in the beginning. I am so sure the others had bets. How could they not, with our track record. I know there were times you wanted to kill me, and yes, there were times I wanted to kill you. You would freak when I kidded about the "pillowing". You would get this puzzled look on your face and look at me saying, "would you do that"? Yeah right mom, don't sleep on your back. I finally had you in my life in a positive way, I wasn't going to blow it by pillowing you.

You and I were so different from each other. Like cooking eggs for instance, you and I were light years apart. I had this thing about eating an egg that was still alive. You said I killed them. I thought we were avoiding ptomaine. I'm sure you would correct me on that. "It's not ptomaine you jackass it's salmonella", "Jesus, what are you learning in that college"?, laughing the entire time. You had a way when you said "Jackass". There was such expression to it. You made people smile at the thought of themselves being a jackass. Horses ass was another good one. Anyway, since my expertise in cooking was in the drive- thru category, trying to cook for someone who cooked as well as you did was, pretty scary. Not only did I fail egg 101, but pasta done, adente has new meaning, and boy did you let me know that one. The worst part of that episode was that the pasta I was making was those three-minute noodle soups. A kinder death would have been from pillowing I'm sure, after trying to eat that. You really were nice about it. You gave it back to me, kept making faces and told me you were full. I knew your appetite was poor, but I knew it wasn't that poor. Our menu became very limited, pre-made and microwaveable. A prayer answered for me and a decent meal for you, life really is wonderful. Once I learned to take the plastic off the stuff before heating it, we had it made. I tried mom, I really did, and I knew you knew that. You suffered meal after meal very graciously. Thanks...

I am so grateful my cooking didn't kill you. I would still be looking for a country to find refuge in, if it had. I wouldn't have stood a chance in this family if they thought my cooking killed you. It would have given them another excuse to disown me, not that some of them ever needed an excuse to ignore my existence. At least they're consistent about some things. I know if you were here, most of what is going on now wouldn't be going on. You know when dad died, stuff ruffled and you shut us all up. When you left, it felt like life had been snatched from my very existence. There was no one now to still the children. Emotions were rampant, adults became weeping children. That very special aura mothers carry and dispel, sometimes never even having to utter a word, was gone forever. None of us knew what to do. They will never admit it but no one was sure of anything at that point. You know when dad died, I was very sad; when you left, something in me changed forever. You were a major anchor in my life. Even though most of my life I did on my own, I could always call you after the fact or before the fact. Either way you gave me your opinion and no matter how many times I wanted to say, "I disagree", I learned to listen with care knowing no matter what, that you were still my mother. That what you said mattered, and then turn around and did what ever I thought was better as I had done since childhood. I guess I never grew up in that way. Now I wonder how many times you wanted to say, "told you so", but kept your mouth shut. It makes me smile when I think about how many things I thought I got over on you and dad. Daddy was street smart and you were book smart. You have an awful lot of secrets with you don't you. Perhaps in time, from the loose lips of others, I will learn of some of my antics I thought you never knew about, but really did. It'll make me laugh. Then I'll spend a copious amount of time trying to figure out how you knew, blaming sisters, brothers, friends, or neighbors for telling on me; never giving credit to you and dad for doing similar things as floundering adolescents. I remember when I was writing a paper towards my degree, I called you on the phone and asked you a question about something way back in history, and you answered the question without hesitating. I was dumbfounded. "How do you know that?" I asked you in awe. You replied without a thought, "Because we didn't smoke pot when I went to school". Oh, oh. I thought quietly to myself. Did you know? How, the hell did you know we did that. I couldn't speak. You Laughed. Daddy was also good at confusing the hell out of us by asking weird questions regarding what we had been up to. Before we knew it, we were dead. You could never retrace what you had said to him before he confused you. Then somehow you told a semi-truth about what you had been up to and then you were really dead. He could not have done what I did, so how did he know I did it? When I think about it now I think it was the face of fear. Once daddy said, "Come'ere you, I want to talk to you". Fear burst out all over your face, instantly. Dead, without a word. I guess dad has many secrets with him too. But you like grama have plenty more secrets than he does. From your own lifetime and then the one you had with us. There are things that I will never know about you, and there are things you will never know about me. It's supposed to be that way. Respect for a parent and secrets from childhood and adulthood for me. Nothing wrong with that. It's probably a lot safer that way. Although, now a days kids know a lot more about their parents and speak freely of it, than were ever even allowed to think. We had obvious boundaries. Somehow, we knew better than to ask certain things. I don't think I ever wanted to know much. Just how to get the

hell out of there. I know subconsciously, that must
have been a priority for me. I used to walk to
school real slow hoping to be kidnapped on the
way. Bet you didn't know that one, did you. I
guess, I was never kidnapped because you always
told me never to get in a car with a stranger. You
now know why I had all those late notes, some
signed and some forged. How did you find those
notes anyway? I think I was just an easy nail. You
could read me like a book, right up to the end. You
knew when I was hurt, or pissed off. You just
didn't know what to do about it all the time. But
sometimes you would come up with some real
cool stuff, and I'd be dumbfounded. The woman
who hates mush just moved the earth with mush.
I'd be speechless and you'd yell, "Are you
listening to me?" What the hell are you doing over
there, spacing out on me". "Mary pay attention".
All I could manage was a "what". You were full
of surprises, while you were getting ready to
leave.

You proved us all wrong so many times. We all thought we knew what was best for you and you knew we thought that. Somehow that thing mothers have, you know that thing you had, that always gave you the goods on what we were talking about kicked in and you were telling us all where to go. You were "rowing your own boat" as you said often and that was that. You fought like hell to keep your life, your way. When you finally did give in, you did it with great finesse. You just stopped doing something you could no longer do or started doing something that was needed, like the oxygen. And there was not much said about it anywhere. Not a lot of people knew you weren't driving anymore. Your last good drive kept you out most of the day. It nearly gave me a heart attack. I was worried sick. You went out to your favorite bookstore some twenty odd miles away. You never even said you were going out, you just up and left. You came home exhausted, but happy. That was the last time you drove your beautiful car and you never said a word about it. It was just over. You surprised me just about everyday, I was so proud of you. I used to tell you that a lot before you left. Sometimes you heard me, sometimes you didn't. It was not until you got sick that I could tell you that. I am sorry it took so long for me to tell you. In the rule of your realm and of our time together, I was no angel and you were no saint; but there were plenty of times, I was proud of you. I was just too into toughness, to say anything. I mean mom, I had an image to protect. No way in hell was I going to say something nice about a parent in front of a friend. But, if a friend said something derogatory about either you or dad, I kept true to my tough image. In the end, it was you who had something to protect. Your motherhood, your pride, what little self esteem you had, and your dignity. No person living or dead was going to tell you how to do anything. You were rowing your own boat and you were doing a great job. I really was proud of you, ask anybody. As an adult far from where I once was, it felt cool to be proud of you. As your daughter, it was wonderful. You were able to give me a lot before you left. Some of it you will never understand; all of it will stay within me, through eternity. That's a given. Why did you wait a lifetime to stand so tall? I am sorry for you. I, because of you, am able to right some wrongs before they happen. I could be you all over again and I suppose in some ways I am a lot like you and damn proud of it. Then too there are some things I fight. Only because I can sometimes feel what pain you went through and I know I could never handle it.

The physical and emotional pain I watched you endure towards the end was heartbreaking. I learned early on to shut up and get the aspirin. You believed in your heart that if you gave into

the pain, you were giving into another demon of
the cancer. The oxygen was bad enough,
according to you. You got pretty good at rolling
the tubing into a ball and throwing it across the
porch. You sat in your chair in terrible pain. You
would ask me for aspirin and tell me to shut up
before I got to say anything. It was hard to shut
up. You were in such pain but I shut up. You were
still the mommy. I wanted you to stay the
mommy. As time was passing us by, little by little
I was doing for you, all the things you once did for
me. You and I got over the uneasiness of semi role
reversal softly. We eased into things, never
acknowledging we were both in places we were
terrified of. I was aware not to say "let me do that
for you" or "I'll do that mom" and you very
rarely said "Could you do this for me". I guess it
was mostly imagination that I was caregiver and
you were the care getter. Whatever it was, I
believe in my heart that it worked. It wasn't easy
was it? I know there were times you wanted to

put your foot up my ass, but you didn't. Years
ago, you just would have put your foot up my ass.
Years ago I would have just up and left.

The hardest thing for me to keep my mouth
shut about was your pain. I could not fathom it.
The colon cancer had spread to your uterus. Your
uterus was collapsing from the cancer. I never
tried so hard in my life to come up with a way to
ease pain as when I tried to think of ways to ease
your pain. Of course every once in a while I stuck
a "mom let me call the doctor" and you would
shut me up. It was one of the only things I felt
helpless about with you. Most other things, as
time went on, you just conceded to. Of course,
when you finally wanted me to do something for
you, I got so nervous I was like a bull in a china
shop. How many times I narrowly missed
sucking your oxygen tubing up that super sucker
of a vacuum you had. All you wanted me to do
was get the crumbs up from your lunch. You had
a funny sounding scream.

You are the only person I know who could scream and get any person around when you screamed, to do the same. And that little jump you did, you know the one. You actually became airborne, swearing to God in a split second. You were an easy scare. And I am swearing that I never scared you on purpose. Your hearing deficit made you an easy scare. I remember walking in just saying "hi" and you'd be flying up in the air. It must have been very frustrating for you. Not able to hear most common sounds. I know how frustrated I would become at your not answering me, I can't imagine your frustration at not hearing half of what I said. I know it wasn't funny but mom some funny things occurred because of your shortchanged sense of hearing. A waiter in a restaurant asked you if you would like an appetizer, "I'll have a scotch and water" was your reply. I used to cry laughing not at you but when we would get disconnected while on the phone. I would try to call you back only to get a busy signal, I knew you didn't know I wasn't there anymore. Helen recently told of the time daddy made an obscene phone call to you. You were both out in the back porch and dad had gotten his first cell phone. He waited for the perfect time to dial your home number. When the phone rang, he said he didn't feel like getting up, could you get it. You went and got it and he started his heavy breathing and talking stupid. When you screamed, " Tom get out here in the kitchen someone's talking dirty to me on the phone", daddy almost croaked from laughter. Only daddy could come up with something like that and make it work.

You despised your phone. Almost as bad as you despised the TV remote. You could sew intricate stitches on material but you could not hang up the portable phone in one shot nor could you get the remote to respond to your command. You watched an entire day of sewing shows in Spanish closed caption because you could not get the hang of the menu on the remote. I am safe to say now mom, patience was not one of your virtues. You could put those teeny weenie batteries in your hearing aid with no problem but you always had problems with the phone and the remote. I do remember you were very proud of yourself when you finally figured out the Spanish and English thing. I have your last remote, it's there in your chair. Every once in a while I smile, when I see it, sometimes I cry.

I don't know what happened to your phone. I do have the tape recording of your outgoing message, from your answering machine. I Remember right after you left calling your number just to hear your voice, it wasn't to be heard. Your phone was disconnected almost immediately after you left. From what I've heard I was not the only one who was calling to hear your voice. People were not happy to hear a stranger say, "the number you have reached"...they wanted to hear you. You were gone. That unlisted number you had, that most everyone in the

Continental United States knew by heart, was disconnected forever. Mom, people really called to hear your voice. There was nothing special about your voice, except that it was yours. An awful lot of people loved you, I wish that you will know that wherever you may be. I know you never believed it while you were here.

The way some of your own treated you, probably made it very difficult for you to believe there was any love for you. You carried so much unnecessary guilt with you throughout your life. You told me things that I was amazed about. My instinct was to kick some ass. I told you how I felt. We had some pretty lengthy conversations. I feel guilty about some things in my life but not about who I am. The guilt you felt for who you had been was so sad. You had no idea how to forgive yourself for things you said or did way back when. You were not in your right mind or heart when you were drinking confidence from re-useable peanut butter jars. Who would be? No self esteem, seven kids, little or no money. At the time I was unforgiving. I couldn't help it; neither could they. Somehow some of them never let it go, perhaps they never will. You worked hard at leaving in peace; I watched and listened as you did it. I hope wherever it is you may be, that you are flying on your own. Mom, you paid the piper, you deserve to soar.

Whoops mush sorry, back to gadgets. Your house had the best. The pepper grinder with the headlight blew my mind. On the hour, one could hear birds chirp, a lighthouse clang its bell, a dog bark and beautiful chimes from an anniversary clock. Your hearing deprived you of the sounds heard on the hour. The best was when the batteries in the bird clock were dying. I laughed my ass off. You couldn't hear it, you yelled for me to stop laughing at your house. I couldn't stop laughing, the birds were chirping in slow motion. There was also some kind of dog bone that barked when it felt like it. No one knew where the damn thing was. It was just there. I remember when dad died, everyone wanted a toy. I just saw a little girl playing with the bear that hung between your dining room and the kitchen for eons of time. It hangs between the kitchen and dining room at Sean's house. Very appropriate, I think. Your house had character, mom, I miss being there. There was something about walking in that front door. The stairway wall was lined with pictures of everyone when they all only had one chin. Straight thru to your cozy kitchen, it was best room in the house. Tea pots everywhere, holding remnants of comfortable conversations. Four generations have passed through the rooms of your house and everyone of those people at one time or another sat at your kitchen table and solved one or more problems of the world. We were also able to create quite a few within our own world. Your house was home. It was still the only place where you could put your feet on the couch and get yelled at. Most of the others didn't have time to sit on their own couches at home. It was the only place where you could go and see everybody at the same time. At least those who were talking to each other. It was the only place you could go to get the "dirt" on family gossip. It was the only place you could go to get "ranked" on and get it over with all at once. Yep, your house had character. And it helped develop quite a few characters. It's just too bad some of those characters have chosen to jump from pages of a menacing novel. I am sorry that your leaving gave some people the belief that they could do what they wanted and it wouldn't matter because you weren't here to quell their meanness and hatred from ignorance. Not that you could do that so well but they were careful most times about what they said and did when you were around. Your leaving opened the floodgates for some of the most incontestable acts of stupidity I have ever witnessed. Nothing proven by any of it. Except mom, that you were a lot more than you thought you were in a lot of ways. You were a very powerful woman. You kept the troops in somewhat of a line. Without you, most of the troops aren't troops anymore, I'm sorry mom. Some people spoke their peace but it fell on deaf ears.

I don't know that you should worry so much though mom. Just as it has done   before, time will heal some wounds. Some of us will surface a little closer than we are now but then too there are some things that will never heal. I am making that choice with no regrets mom. I did not deserve what happened. I know you tried to catch my broken heart with both hands. I could feel you through the people who do love me. You must know mom, the love you and I taught each other before you left was the greatest love of all. Nothing and no one can ever take that from me. No one person on earth should ever think that they can.

I know how much you wanted things to be okay before you left. You wanted those renounced siblings to be forgiven and treated as they should have been all along, respectfully. It was all you really wanted, the love crap could come later, if ever. I thought it was almost going to work. A few hours after you left I watched and the family was actually behaving and treating each other with care. Then within hours one person true to his nature shattered it. He helped destroy what could have been just what you always wanted. What a horse's ass. I suppose that's why, in my dreams I pray you are nestled in peace, far from the places you left behind. I don't ever remember you wanting a lot, except for spaghetti. One thing I know you wanted was for all of us to get along. Helen spoke of that, right after you left. The listeners fell silent. Like I said before, it fell on deaf ears. I'm not sure that it could ever happen. True to the Irish heritage we are so proud of, this family always fought and will continue to fight like hell. There will always be some misguided by the misguided and then there

will be those who are banished to boogey land.
What you wanted was insurmountable. Not
because it is impossible but because of selfishness.
There is so much of it. Maybe because we had so
little of everything when we were growing up,
that whatever we have now we don't want to
share. Especially love. The hate runs deep in
some people. Scary that they would be family.
Sad, really sad, for you that things turned out the
way they did. Please don't take it to heart mom.
Most of the time life is chock full of choices. Most
of your children are capable of getting along, they
just choose not to. They prefer to blame it on one
thing or another. What cracks me up is that not
one person in this family can afford to throw even
one stone. Some of them practice the art of ass
kissing. One says jump, the other asks how high?
You and I had a hearty conversation about kissing
ass. I cannot and will not do it. You told me if I
didn't learn how to, I would never get anywhere

in life. I am where I am, and where I am is it. I'm pretty okay with it.

You know mom, sometimes you took too much responsibility away from the true causes. I remember when we were talking about how someone was behaving like a horse's ass. You being the mommy tried to take the blame for the jackass who was acting like a horse's ass. I said to you, all the while my knees knocking "Betty Boop, you're good but your not that good." Oh shit what did I just do. I said that aloud. You didn't open your mouth, and I was afraid to move. When I could breath again I remember looking to run like hell. You were cool mom. You just nodded your head. I don't know if you heard me and I don't know what you were thinking. I would like to think that you heard me and knew what I meant by what I said. But knowing you, you were saying, "what is this jackass talking about"? In honesty mom, I think you knew what I meant. It was so hard for you to accept that you were not to blame for all the craziness of the family and the world. I think sometimes you confused the word guilt with Irish Catholic. Not to worry mom you are not alone. Jewish women have the same problem although they don't call it Irish Catholic.

One of the things you talked about was Gus. You asked me out right if he sexually molested or abused us. I was going under the table on this one. Thirty-five years after the fact I was going to get in trouble about something I long since wanted to forget about. It wasn't just me. I was sure of one other whom he molested or abused. I could not believe we were having this conversation. You calmly said. "I should have known. I should have asked you guys back then I should have done something." I'm still looking to go under the table on this one. I just managed to whimper a little "how could you do something if you didn't know what was going on." Please God make the phone ring or something. Neither of us said another word. We sat there, you sullen with your guilt, and me choking on my fear.

Mom, you have nothing to be guilty about unless you knew, and did nothing. And I doubt that. He took us to movies and parks and places you couldn't. He got us out of your hair. And I remember he was a smooth operator, mom. He could fool anybody. Besides, in those days one was forbidden to go near strangers, he was a friend of the family. He had it made. He was good, mom. He covered all his bases. You could not have known unless you asked. I don't ever remember you asking. I doubt I would have told you about it anyway. I was scared to tell you and scared of not telling you. So until you brought it up recently I stayed scared with it. But by then I really didn't care much about it. I am sure by now he has been in trouble for messing with others. My only regret is that, I missed the hanging.

When I think back on all the things you and daddy went through it makes me wonder how the hell you guys did it. You did not kill any of us. Although sometimes you could have. The standard joke right now from you would be that you drank a lot, and daddy slept a lot. No argument there but we are all still here. All somewhat successful and totally dysfunctional as a family. When you look around today we are not so far out of the norm, so Betty Boop, you really did okay with what you had. Which wasn't much. Whether they know it or not they have all survived the way you did. You worked your ass off, did what you could with what you had and survived raising eight kids. You and dad survived and so did we. You know mom, growing up poor Irish Catholic was not the worst thing that could have happened to us. We could have been poor, and ugly.

I could never imagine it being anything else than the way it was growing up in our house. A lot of things happened that hurt you tremendously but we were kids and did not quite get it yet. Just as we had to stay away from some of the people in the neighborhood, so did some people have to stay away from us. We stayed away because they were rogues of a sort or not good company. They stayed away from us because we didn't have the clothes or the clean hands and faces that they thought we should have had. I know that hurt you terribly. You were embarrassed in more ways than one. But mom, we had more fun than their kids had. Our yard had the best dirt in the neighborhood. Growing up with little is probably what makes dreamers, survivors.

You were a very proud woman. I never really knew that. I don't think you ever really let it show until after daddy died. After we all found our "thing" and left the roost, you spent most of your time attending him. He was more work than all eight of us kids put together. He never really "came back" after that aneurysm way back when. But long before he even got sick with that aneurysm in his aorta, he had to be the laziest man both physically and emotionally that God ever put on this earth. He was the best provider you could want but you never wanted to ask him to move over on the couch. I believe in my heart that he stifled you. He did it with guilt. And you being the person you were couldn't help yourself. And yet you crawled on your hands and knees up fourteen steps every night to be in your bed. How you did that every night and yet you were unable to defend yourself against him for all those years. It's not that dad was a bad person, he could just be very, very mean at times. The strength you could muster for the trip upstairs amazed me and scared me. There was no way in hell you were going to sleep downstairs on the couch. Remember. You'd say, "Ready"? I'd look over and you'd be antsy to get up. Once moving you didn't stop till you got to the steps. I'd get the tubing ready and up you would go on all fours, cursing or praying all the way up to the top. Once up at the top, you would pause, always pleading for breath. Sometimes I know I tried to pretend to myself that I couldn't hear you gasping for air. Most times I would just try not to cry. Rowing your own boat, you were, and proud as peacock doing it. There were times I felt like you rowing your own boat was going to be the death of me. I didn't understand, until I watched you leave. I am so very proud of you mom. I am certain that a lot of people could not pull off what you did. You did it the way you wanted to do it. And you did it with such grace. It was damn near perfect mom.

Right to the very end it went the way you wanted it to go. So many times on a downer day, you would start with you were ready to go stuff and you wanted to go already and you didn't want to live like this anymore. I would try not to cry. But you know some how as time went on, I felt myself understanding more and more about your wanting to go already. I remember one time even getting up the nerve to ask if you were sure

you were ready. It was harder than when I asked
you where you wanted to be when it was near
time to go. To the latter you said. "Here in my
house if it's okay with the doctor". And then roar
like a lion: "I don't want to talk about it anymore."
"I'm going to get better any how." How many
times you said that. You had choices this time
around with the cancer. You always talked that
you were grateful the surgery never happened.
You believed you would never have lasted as long
as you did, had they done what they set out to do.
You wanted nothing to do with "their" cancer
treatment. You did it all the first time around.
Now you were going to do it on your own terms.
No Chemo, no Radiation, for a very long time not
even oxygen. And not until two days before you
left, nothing for the pain, except aspirin. You gave
new meaning to "stubborn Irish". You did agree to
see a doctor once in awhile, which was cool. He
was pretty cool wasn't he mom. He said you had a
lot of guts, so did his nurses. You liked him for

that. The first doctor you had seen or liked in thirty years. He was really good to us mom, he really was. There was never any kind of hassle with him. He did whatever you two agreed on. It was pretty cool that you trusted him. He was so kind at the end.

He was amazed that you always looked so good. It really was hard to believe at times that you were so sick. You put make-up on everyday no matter what. I remember the day you didn't. It was the day before you left. That stubborn Irish thing. It worked for you. You were walking around until the day before you left. What I think worked for you sometimes too, was your denial fits. Every once in a while you would tell me that the cancer was gone or that maybe you never had it in the first place. That it was going to get better. I guess you needed to do that. In the beginning I almost believed you were going to be okay. I tried with all my heart to listen to you wanting to go do this and go do that. I wanted to believe you in the worst way. Stranger things have happened. You wanted to walk around the block. All the time. You just wanted to walk around the block. I said I would go with you. We never went. Thank God, I don't know about you, but I never would have made it. I had no idea sometimes if I should have encouraged you or discouraged you. I'd say, " Okay lets go". You'd say, "Are you trying to get rid of me"? If I said, "I don't think you should try that mom". You'd say "I'm not dead yet you know"! Here we go again.

I wonder sometimes if your denial at times gave you strength. I kept thinking if you thought you weren't sick and you were going to be alright why were you fighting so hard not to be sick. You tried so hard not to be sick, you really did. You know mom, when I changed physically, I changed emotionally big time. After the accident I had no idea what was going to happen to me. In a split second of time I went from a healthy two legged person, to one who can only dream of running across a parking lot. When you got sick there was some awesome changes in you emotionally. A person can't help but change when the odds are suddenly stacked against them. You and I changed for the better. Both of us were tested to the maximum of "What the hell happened". Some days you were different than others. The days when you felt like taking on the world, you did. I never saw you do anything "because of the situation". You did the things you wanted to do, put your foot in your mouth more than once and pretty much went along as you wanted. The difference was the struggle, physically. That frustrated the hell out of you. Your physical body was malfunctioning and it drove you nuts. You would fidget in your chair trying to find a comfortable position to sit. Towards the end, you couldn't stand for any length of time. Your frustration would turn to anger but I have to say this mom, you really didn't come across that angry for what was bestowed on you. It seemed to me

that you were angrier throughout your life than
you were going through this one last nightmare.
Funny thing, when you did get mad, I got scared.
When you got scared, I got brave. When you
cried, so did I. And boy did you hate to cry. It was
so hard to see you cry. Watching your mother cry
does something to you deep down inside. I
wanted to defend you in any way I could. I
wanted to make you okay. I wanted to make you
all better. I wanted to cry like a baby. I know it
took an awful lot to make you cry. Never mind to
cry in front of someone. I knew I had to stay in
my place when you cried. So many times I wanted
to hold you. But I knew by now, if I reached to
comfort you, you'd wipe your tears and go back to
doing something else. I could sneak a shoulder
hug once in a while, with a kiss to your forehead
and you would smile. You had such a beautiful
smile.

I liked it when we got you tucked in bed at
night. I would push the hair back on your

forehead and kiss and tell you I loved you. You'd say, "I love you too". Then you would take a book and read yourself to sleep. I would come back up two or three times more in the night to check on you. You would laugh if you were awake. Nighttime was my cry time. It was then; I could talk to myself, cry to grama and wish that none of this was happening. I had no idea in the world how to do what we were doing. I had taken a course or two while I was in school but this was the real thing. There's not a book written that could tell me how to lay my mother down softly to die. It wasn't supposed to be this way mom. You were supposed to grow old and grouchy. You were supposed to stay to be a pain in the ass. You were supposed to become a burden. You were supposed to become the topic of conversation at your children's dinner tables. You know the ones where everyone complains about an elderly parent. Instead, life threw us a curve and you became my hero.

In the beginning you had a hard time about having me there to help you. I eased my way into your life again. First by days, then weekends. Then, I was there. You kept insisting you didn't need any help with anything. I knew you were fibbing when you couldn't empty the dishwasher. I tried hard not to make you an invalid. That was really hard. I wanted to do everything for you, then so did you. More than once we spoke about your embarrassment at my helping you with some things. You were my mother. You had me, raised me and you were stuck with me. What happened between the walls of your house during these times would go no further. What the hell would I remember anyway? You and I had a silent pact. I out of respect and admiration for you and you out of pride and newfound trust, kept your needing and my assists between us. At times this made it difficult when someone called to see how you were doing. When you said fine and I said not well, I being the person I am in some of the family's eyes, came out being somewhat of a fraud. What was I doing there if you were okay? What was I trying to do? Was I getting something they weren't going to get? Damn straight I was. Most will never know what it was I got from you. You know mom, I will never understand why they said what they said. You are my mother. From the day I was born I gave you every inch of grief I could and not always on purpose. I owed you life, so why wouldn't I want to be there for you now that yours was ebbing away.

Who was going to bug you like I could bug you? Who could get you pissed off easier? Not any of them. I was good at it and you loved it. You knew I wasn't going anywhere no matter what we got into. I couldn't run away anymore. I only have one good leg. I know both of us thought we were winning at our attempted arguments at one time or another. The longest running argument we had was probably the one about your not needing any help. You were forever trying half to get rid of me. You thought I had a life, like the others. I was lucky, I didn't. I could never have imagined you being alone at times. I know you needed your "whatever time" and I tried to give it to you. I had "whatever time" too and I used to try to do something that kept us both out of trouble. Of course it didn't always work out that way. Remember when I raked the leaves in the backyard and lost my glasses. You and Helen found them after we dumped about eight bags of leaves back on the lawn. Remember when I moved the old air conditioner and hurt my leg. You were telling me not to move it and I was telling you I could move it. When I couldn't get off the couch later, you tried to put cream on my leg but you couldn't get out of the chair. We laughed like crazy. Sometimes you had to help me and then it was like the blind leading the blind. But at least we laughed about it. I guess I was there to keep you on your toes. You were on your toes until the day before you left.

You wanted the strangest things done as time became more precious. For thirty years you wanted the bathroom window molding fixed. We did it together. Such a simple thing made you happy. And it made me crazy. I couldn't understand what the hell could be so important as bathroom window molding. Weren't there more things you wanted than that, yes, molding cut for the cellar door. The molding was cut for the door but it never got installed. You had to leave before we got the chance to fix it. Funny, something that seemed so simple has stayed on my mind since you left. If those two things were so simple to do, why didn't daddy ever do them? Perhaps it was just too simple. Another thing you cracked me up about was the curtains for the kitchen windows. The biggest thing was having the windows cleaned. Not a month before you left, you designed and sewed your curtains for the kitchen. Foolishly I tried to help you put them up. But not before we searched the ads in the paper for someone to come and do the windows. You were a fanatic about the windows. The house was three stories high. Who looked at the windows? "I do damn it, I can't stand dirty windows, it looks like hell". Our front lawn is "grass grown out of sympathy grass" and you think they can see the dirt on the windows. Anyway, I did the kitchen windows as best I could. As soon as the sun started to set, you could see I failed windows 101. You let me know it too. We searched the ads again finding a name we would call as soon as we got around to it. The curtains were one of the funniest things we tried to do. Somehow, if you pulled a string, which you had sewn into the fabric, the curtain would become a café curtain or something of that nature. One went up great. It was the second one that was a trip. We got it up, you told me to pull the string, I pulled the string and the entire curtain came apart. I pulled the wrong string. I didn't hear any yelling. I was scared to death. I was afraid to look in your direction. I didn't hear anything, I looked and there you were trying not to collapse with laughter. You thought I was going to have a fit of rage and I thought you were going to kill me. Nothing happened. You redid the curtain. We hung it and that was that. The windows never did get cleaned. The curtains really looked good. You felt really good about getting that done. I truthfully couldn't see how you were going to be able to do those curtains but you did them. We just took it a little bit at a time and we did them. You were so proud, it was so cool. It really was. You loved your kitchen. Some great decisions were made at that table. You spent hours doing your crossword puzzles by the sunlight that made it through what you thought were the dirty windows. Somehow everyone always ended up in the kitchen. It wasn't a big room by any means. It was a perfect square perhaps ten feet by twelve feet at the most. Remember in the olden days when we had that little gas stove. You used to bake bread in that blue dish. That was the best. You made pancakes on that cast iron griddle. We had huge double sinks deep enough to give the baby a bath in. Daddy would get up early sit and have his coffee and listen to his weather radio. To fish or not to fish?

He got the hell out of there before you got up. If it was a fish day he had to get out before you thought of something to be done. There was always something that needed to be done. He just took off to make sure you couldn't ask him to do anything. You were pretty fair with him about fishing. He told you he had to go fishing, it was to put food on the table. A fabled guilt trip if ever there was one. Every fisherman since St. Peter says the same thing. Remember the time you drove him to the docks with his boat. He got off all right and when you waved frantically at him he waved happily back at you. He was on his way to fish for the day, with your car keys in his pocket. I don't remember how you got home but I know you never went out in your nightgown in the car again. He would clean his fish in your kitchen, leaving fish residue everywhere. He was too tired from fishing to clean up the mess. Then of course we had to bury the fish heads under the rose bushes. We had lousy grass and dirty windows but we had the most beautiful roses around. Always some on your kitchen table. I miss hanging around at your kitchen table. It seemed everyone just ended up in your kitchen. It was one of the smallest rooms in the house but an awful lot went on in there. Cooking, homework, fighting, dishes, phone calls it all happened there, for whatever reason the lighting was good and minor surgeries like splinter removal or fish hook removal were done in there too. It was always "come in the kitchen", maybe because you spent most of your life in there. You put your foot down when daddy tried to start doing his woodworking on the table. Before you left, it was too painful for you to sit in there anymore. Towards the end you weren't in there at all except to just pass through getting up in the morning or going up to bed at night.

In my lifetime I never thought that your house, the one I grew up in just as you did, would become a memory so quickly. No matter what happened I always felt like I could come home and I always did. And you were always there. Sitting in your window chair watching the world go by or keeping tabs on Sean while he cut the sympathy grass. I hear people talk of going back to old neighbor hoods and the houses they grew up in all the time. They speak fondly and get melancholy about "what it was like" when they went back. I never thought about it, I always thought your house, with you in it, would be home forever. My place to go is gone and not just because you left. After you left, I was cursed at, thrown out and locked out all within a matter of hours. Have you been back there at all? Just thought I'd ask.

I pass by when I go to Sean and Terri's.
Sometimes I stop and just look at it. It looks
different. The inside shutters are closed tight and
the shades are drawn. You can tell there's no one
there any more. There's no sense of welcome,
anywhere to be seen. There's no echo's of life
coming through the windows. It looks so different.
It's so stilled. I miss you. The funniest thing
happened mom. Remember that dust outline on
the wall in the back porch where a picture had
once hung. They were investigating amongst
themselves as to what could have happened to
whatever it was that was there. Had they come
any time before, they would have known the
picture was gone, months before you left. Helen
and I dug up the two rose bushes. Yours and
Grama's. They are alive and blooming in Seattle.
You would have been proud of us, the way we got
them out of there. Helen was quite nervous during
our rose bush transfer, she kept asking me what to
do if some one came, I told her to swing wide with

the shovel. The local police knew us and liked us better anyway. They knew us from years back. We really had nothing to worry about. The roots to those rose bushes were incredible. All those fish heads paid off. I'm glad she has them.

Those last few weeks sure were hot ones weather wise weren't they mom. It was difficult to finding ways of staying cool. We did all right though with that little a/c in the back porch and putting up the vertical blind in the doorway. I hated that damn thing. It went whatever way it wanted to no matter which way you turned the stupid stick. If you walked through it, it held onto you till you got half way through the kitchen. Sometimes, I would see you flagging your arms all over the place and the slats would go flying, I tried not to laugh. If I did the same thing, you had a holy fit that I was wrecking the place. I used to try and split them down the middle when I knew you were coming. "What are you doing"? "Don't wreck it". "Look out". You couldn't do it either.

The heat really was something else though. And you had to give me a hard time, every time I asked you to drink water. "I hate water". How the hell can you hate water? Its just water. But you hated it. You went into your little kid mode when I asked you more than once to please drink some. Sometimes you even stuck your tongue out at me. I was afraid at that point. You were hardly eating at all. Your not eating brought me to the scariest reality of my life. After the second full day of you snubbing even your favorite, tuna on a roll, I knew you were getting ready to leave. But you still had the strength to bitch about my water lecture. As you weakened, I somehow became our fearless leader. You went along with most whatever I said and finally let me care for you without any boundaries. I tried with all I had to cuddle you with the love and respect you deserved as my mother and to show you that you could trust me, as your life that was waning right in front of us. Everything turned so precious. It seemed to happen so fast. We were going along slowly and then from nowhere, slowly became a tremendous effort. You were so tired. Climbing the fourteen steps to bed became almost impossible. I was happy if you had half a cup of coffee, never mind the water. You would come down from up stairs and sit right on the couch. You started to take more "naps" then ever. The color of your beautiful skin was becoming paler by the day but the eminence of your skin tone never never lessened, you were a real looker mom. You worried about your skin all the time. There was no need to. Your beauty was still intact. It was the rest of you that was coming to the end. The heart that you tried so fervently to show love with and the natural beauty you came into this world with will stay alive in me for a long time to come. I think about you so much. The world outside didn't stop when you left. It felt like it did but it really didn't. It was our little world that stopped. You were there for me when I came into the world not yet ripe enough and I was there for you when you left the world, pretty much already to go. Pretty cool.

I could not have asked for a greater gift in my life, than the time I spent with you. Truly I was the runt of the litter, probably causing you more grief than you deserved. My childhood antics were a slight glimmer of innocence. I don't think I ever really got in trouble on purpose, no one does. No kid ever thinks they're going to get caught at anything, just as they think they are infallible in speeding cars and reckless adventures. I think I spent a good deal of my youth believing that you didn't like me. You loved me because I was your daughter but I think it was hard for you to like me. I know being the first-born girl, I was not exactly what you had in mind. I was difficult from the beginning. When I gave you a hard time, daddy used to tell me about how you would go to the hospital everyday to see me in the incubator after I was born. I need you to know that I did not spend those last seven weeks with you because I felt guilty about the childhood antics. I spent that time with you because for no one, did I have a greater love for. As I grew emotionally and chronologically over time, I became more aware of your feelings, your hurt, and some of your misguided ideas. Life was teaching me and it was from just that teaching that I realized it was all done without instructions, by trial and error, tears and sorrow. You raised eight kids and one husband alone. There was never anyone there to ease your burdens or wipe your tears. Even by chance if there were someone there, it was difficult for you to accept their love. Before you left I know deep in my heart that you knew how I loved you and I know you loved me and yes even liked me. How else could it have been that we could have laughed so much in the face of what was happening. You were comfortable with me, you trusted me, you cried with me and all that mom, was the greatest gift you could have given me before you left.

By the way, thank you for sending the bracelet. I cannot fathom that it would be a coincidence that I would receive a bracelet I had given you thirty years ago on the day my best friend Colin would succumb to brain cancer. Yeah mom for the second time in less than a year, as you well know, a part of me has died. My heart has come unraveled and my soul searches once again for some kind of peace. When the bracelet fell out of its wrapping into the palm of my hand, I thought I was going to faint. There etched on a single tarnished gold charm were the words; *MOM, LOVE MARY, 1973.* Such a great comfort could only have come from up above. I knew then that Colin would be well taken care of and so would you. The bracelet was found amongst your things and Kathy and Mike thought I would like to have it. Funny thing Kathy related how mailing the bracelet kept getting delayed, by both her and by anyone else she asked to mail it. Makes you really wonder. So many times while Colin was sick I wanted to call you. When he died, I wanted to call you. Instead, you touched me with the bracelet. So many times just for no reason I wanted to call you, just as I had always done before. Little things in life mean so much. Thank you for helping me know that.

II

Much time has past since I started this letter to you. It seems that time is working against me. The more time that passes, the harder it seems to get. I suppose growing up never gets easy. It wasn't easy then and it's not easy now. Before you left, I wanted to be the sensible daughter taking care of her dying mother. I needed you to know it was alright. That you were safe with me. That I would not allow anything to hurt you anymore. I wanted you to know that you weren't going to die alone. That I would be there with you, if God allowed it. I tried so hard mom. Though deep inside of me, I was the little girl crying out in agony. "MOMMY help me." " Please don't go". "I don't know what to do". How could this be happening? I was scared to death. I took the best care of you I could. I loved you with all my heart. And perhaps that was what gave me the strength to endure the heartache of what would become the greatest loss of my mortal life. You were too young to die and too sick to live. You had a young mind. And your mind was intact up until the night before you left. You were reading your last book that night. Don't worry, it's been returned to the library. You never wanted to give up an inch. You gave that cancer a run for its evilness. When I asked you how you were doing it, you would reply, "I have no choice". How untrue. You had choices and you picked all the right ones mom. Because they were your choices. It took you till your dying days for you to really believe in yourself but you did it. What a wonderful way to go. It showed.

All this is so permanent. There's no see you later anymore. It's such an end. All that goes on are thoughts and tears. Missing, wishing, tears. Sometimes frames of memories race through my mind, allowing a glimpse of you. I do find some peace then. I know you had to go. Your choices were now given to a stronger Being. It was you, who courageously ran out of strength and finally said okay let's go, I'm tired, and I'm ready when you are. You were done rowing. Your tired boat was drifting, safely. You were strong enough now, to let go. You were in good hands. He took you gently. It showed.

When I called your best friend to let her know that you were gone, she said, "Mary, your mother knew. She told me, she was leaving". I wasn't surprised. If it's okay with you mom, I'd like to write about our last week together. I will still be true to my word, I won't tell them everything. My heart at this very moment is crying tender mournful tears. I am sometimes able to truly feel my heart ache, for missing you. I love you...

Monday morning, took way too long. On good days when I brought you your coffee, you made a wisecrack sat up and had your coffee. This day, you were silent and told me you'd drink it later. You were calm, still, and wrapped tightly in your top sheet. "You okay mom"? "I'm fine", "I'm alright". The only word that came to my mind and not on my lips was shit, just shit. Your bed was a huge king size boxing ring. You looked so small in it. You looked so cute laying on your side, semi-cuddling your pillow. Next to you was dad's pillows, his half of the bed, made up neatly, empty. Although more than once you told me you felt him next to you. You wanted to sleep a little more but first needed some aspirin. After you took the aspirin you laid down again, I tucked you in, kissed your forehead and went outside to sit on the deck by the garage. My body convulsed in agonizing sobs. The most fearful reality of my life was here, now engulfing every aching pore of my being. I never felt more helpless in my life. This was the real truth; this was knowing that all that control, it's really left to a higher Being. This was knowing that we are not able to stop the rain, that we are borrowers, of a greater power. I tried so hard to know, that you were going to a better place. It was the only way I knew I could survive what was unfolding before my eyes. It was almost like pretend. I say pretend because I was numbed with fear. I was trying to pretend I wasn't. I knew where you were going because I believe in it with all my heart. It is not pretend, not in any way. At least not to me. I wanted you to go but I wanted you to stay. You were in so much pain. I didn't know which way to pray. For a miracle, to make you all better or for God to take you quickly. When I could finally gather myself, I looked around at all daddy's empty birdfeeders. I was so sad mom. My world as I had known it was changing way beyond my imagination. The other half of my childhood was dying. There wasn't a damn thing I could do about it. I was standing under your favorite cherry tree, that too had seen kinder times. I remember when that tree used to bloom, it was magnificent. A huge orb of white covered part of the backayard, the slightest breeze could carry the cherry blossoms swirling to the ground, so much so, it looked as if it were snowing. Every year for eons of time that tree and our ever-growing footprints carried blossoms and cherry juice across your floors, validating the infancy of Spring. The best "backayard" in the neighborhood. Who was it that said "backayard" instead of backyard anyway? Was it ever who?

It was near nine when I went back up to see what was up. There you were sitting on the side of your bed in your hand your empty coffee cup. "Ready". "No, could you get me another cup of coffee"? Sure. I came back with your coffee. You were now sitting at the end of your bed. "Here ya go Betty BooP". "I'll be back later". Half an hour later I came back and you were on the far side of the bed, just sitting. You got showered and dressed this time around. We didn't say much. The feeling was okay. It wasn't tense or anything like that, it was okay. You wouldn't eat anything once we got down stairs. You got in your chair,

then got up and lay down on the couch. You
wanted aspirin again. Within the hour you got up
and went to your chair. I got you some seltzer and
you put on the TV. You were quiet and at the
same time I knew you were in a really bad mood. I
could hear you curse at the ads on TV, the news
and the weather. You stayed like that most of the
day. Sleeping on the couch a little here and a little
there. Nothing to eat, very little to drink and a
blow out in your broom. Nothing that day was
right. It was just a bad day. I have seen you pissed
off in your day but this day was not a recall. It
was from the pain and you were trying so hard to
fight the physical weakness. Your anger was
justified. You went up early that Monday. It was
still light outside. Your climb this night would be
the hardest you would make. You stopped three
times on the way up. You weren't much help in
the bedtime preparations. Once you settled in, I
hung on the edge of the bed. You said, "I don't
know how much longer I can do this"? "Don't

worry about it mom". I had no idea what to say to you. Neither did you to me. You weren't scared. You were calm. I kissed you on the forehead. You took up your book but you didn't open it. I stayed there for a couple of minutes. You and I sat there in a deafening silence. But I could hear your lungs gasping for air. "Goodnight Betty Boop", "Sleep tight". "Goodnight sweetheart".

I went downstairs. Checked the lock on the front door and went into the kitchen. I sat in your chair at the table. The coffee pot was set up for the morning and the light was on over the stove. I just sat there. Just as I am sitting here now. My mind was thoughtless. Life around the outside of your house went on. I could hear the traffic passing by on the highway. I went to check on you. I made it half way up the stairs when I heard you yell; "I'm alright honey, go to bed". I smiled and went back down, out to the porch. I sat on the couch looking at the muted TV. You know mom, from the very beginning, from the day I came home from school that week of Christmas and listened to your recorded message on my answering machine, nothing was the same. The "taken for granted" time of the days that passed me by, were no longer thoughtless and crammed with frivolous worries. From the moment I spoke with you that December day, nothing was twenty-four hours anymore, nothing was tomorrow. I wanted to leave school to take care of you but you wouldn't hear of it. You were going to be fine. You didn't need anybody to take care of you. We showed you didn't we. When the surgery never happened, you came home and did your thing. No one called me that day. Terry apologized profusely but no one called me to tell me what had happened. That should have been an eye opener to me. Anyway, I guess the only way to sum up what I felt most days until you left, was fear. Some days it was incredible fear. Some days it was numbing. All the while you were saying you were going to be all right. There were times I wanted to scream at you to wake up, you had big time cancer, how the hell did you think you were going to be okay. Had I only known you were faring another courageous lifetime, ever how short it was to be, I would have believed you . But, Jesus, mom it was cancer. It was the second time. The doctors didn't give you much time. But to you, time meant nothing. To me cancer and time were fear, until you drilled it into my head that it was going to be your way. You spoke half-truths about what they said, sometimes even conveniently forgetting what the doctors said. Your defenses were incredible. Your immense denial could very well have been the very thing that kept you alive, for as long as you were. How could you die from something you didn't have? Not only your denial but also your defiance to cancer treatments. No one would have thought that you were doing the right thing, by not doing what they all thought was best for you. How did you know, in this world of modern medicine, what was best for you? This was perhaps the only time in your entire life that you were truly running the show. There was no one who was going to stifle you. You said so many times you had nothing to lose. You were dying. Well, this here was your opportunity to be the free running delinquent you always wanted to be. I knew you had it in you Betty Boop. You let each and everyone of us know what your wishes were. There were no choices for us. It was your boat. And damn didn't you stick to it. Remaining a lady the entire time. We all disagreed at times. We were scared, so were you but no matter, you'd listen to a plea or two and ignore it. When you were damn good and ready, that was all there was to it. When you were damn good and ready.

When I think about the time issue, it remains somewhat bold in my memory. I suppose because it really didn't mean anything in the beginning. They said you had a certain amount of time and you ignored it. It only started to mean something at the very end, the last few days, time

became the essence of everything. I remember
begging God to make the days longer. For the first
time in my life, I dreaded sunrises and sunsets.
Those last few days, nothing had a time frame.
There was no breakfast ,lunch or dinner time
because you weren't eating. There was no
structure to be followed. Everything was now
done on the spur of the moment. I felt like I was
walking on my tip toes, which you know I can't do
but it felt like that . When you wanted something,
I did it as fast as I could do it. I guess I thought it
would make a difference if I did things right away.
I suppose that was my bargain with God, "If I
hurry, could You please take Your time" When I
would put a cool washcloth on your forehead, you
would close your eyes and let a soft moan whisper
from your lips. It was those little things you did,
that let me know you were allowing yourself to be
taken care of and that it felt okay. It also brought
me to the most sorrowful reality of my life. I
remember it all. It travels through my memory

very gently, allowing me glimpses of a precious time, that I pray, never to forget. I am sad at times, though not always. It's those waves that get me. They just come over me, seemingly from nowhere. Sometimes I do search for them, though. There are times I want to think of you on purpose and there are plenty of times, I want to cry, just for the two of us. I mourned for you when you were here, dying, right before my eyes and I am still mourning you. Hell, I still mourn my gold fish that died years ago. I think when you love someone and they leave for greener pastures, you spend a lifetime mourning them in all kinds of compassionate ways. Loves lost to eternity are always with you and with a mere whisper they can appear in your thoughts. But sadly, not in your arms. Truly, they are in your heart and in your memories. And we must always want for more. The wanting will keep them alive in us and just a whisper away. Learning to whisper is a timeless magic, it is healing. That last week we had together, You and I became the women we always had wanted to become. We worked real well together . All that had been, was here before us bolding testing our every strength. How you had raised me was now there, for you to see. How I loved you as my mother was now there for you to feel. I always wanted you to know how much I loved you mom. Your anti-mush made that an arduous challenge. Yet, I knew in the end, that you really believed my love. Thank you.

Tuesday hit me like a ton of bricks. When you said I could call the doctor for pain medicine, I knew we were in trouble. Trouble was obvious. You were weakened something awful from the pain. I remember the conversation. I said "Please mom let me call the doctor to get you something", You interrupted "No god damn it I'll be alright." I just looked at the TV. Not five minutes later you said "What do you think he can give me?" I said. "I don't know." "Something mom, you don't have to be this uncomfortable." I was near tears. "Call him tomorrow". "Why don't I call him now so maybe I can pick it up in the morning instead of waiting." "Alright go ahead". And I called. The doctor had already left for the day. His nurse was a bit miffed by my request for something for pain for you. I explained that my mother was a great BS artist and could fool the best of them. She indicated that the records showed you were doing okay. I then explained where we were in our journey. She was so kind. She offered to call him right away. I thought, rather than get you all excited I would wait until morning. I thanked her for her understanding and assured her I would call back on Wednesday morning. I grabbed the aspirin and fibbed you a bit about my conversation with the nurse. I made you some tea, which seemed to help a little. You ate nothing, and fought with me about the fluids. I was grateful your Mets won that afternoon. It was a hot humid day. The little air conditioner in the porch window worked like hell to keep both you and I comfortable. You were pretty quiet that day. Napping here and there. A couple of times I caught myself checking to see if you were still breathing. You were. I felt so bad. You were really a hurting puppy. It was so sad, so very sad. Feeling powerless, what a reality. This was truth. A bolder one I will not face again until it is my time to go. Everything this day seemed to be larger than life itself. Here we were, seeing and believing what we had been taught throughout our almost Catholic lives, He is in charge. No mortal being can argue. When He is ready for you, it's time to go. Nothing can stop it. Not a pill, a tear, or even a prayer. I felt as though I were up against a brick wall. There was nothing I could do, except to comfort you. And when you weren't looking, cry like a baby.

I felt so small in the scheme of things. I didn't know how to do this. From the beginning I didn't know how to do it. Now it seemed I was even forgetting how to breathe. I couldn't think more than a second ahead. If I tried to, things got loud and scary. I didn't know what it was or when it was that was going to happen. I just knew in my heart that something was coming at me full force. I prayed for strength not to fuck up. That is the only word that could describe it. This was about you. This was how you wanted it to be. You wanted to die here in your house, peacefully. I was going to do everything in my being to make sure it was the way you wanted it to be. I watched you for weeks, probing for peace. You read books, you talked, you cried. You used your rosary beads. You laughed, a lot. And you found it. I saw it. I heard it in your voice and saw it in your eyes. You weren't sad really. Just about missing all of us. I'm not sure there will be a time to miss us. It will be us, who will be missing you. You will be somewhere within all of us, we just have to know that. You are able to reach us through peace and belief. We have not yet reached that utopia. Remember when you would lock yourself in the bathroom for a moments peace. Remember when we learned how to open the lock from the outside with a screwdriver? Remember you wanted a job as a "Lighthouse Keeper" for the peace and quiet and someone found a job for you under "light house keeping". And you were, really going to miss us. Your honesty at the end was more than I could have ever asked for. It is those who did not hear it that are left to wonder, in every sense of the word. I was there to grasp it all, whatever my aching heart could hold, I took it. Because it was here now, in front of me, you were stripped naked of all your lies and you were exposing the you that begged to be free for all those years you were so unfairly and some times innocently oppressed. And all you wanted was to be loved, to be accepted for who you were, in spite of forces who had taken your very soul and buried it beneath a mountain of confusion and sadness. All you needed to do was to love you but it was beyond your reach. You could hear it, you could see it but it never nurtured inside of you. You could never feel it but it was always so close, yours for the taking but lost among so many other twisted innocent beliefs you had within you. Mom if you could only know how we all loved you. Each hard ass in their own way. Funny how daddy always said "I love you" before he hung up the phone. It took you a very long time to say that. But you did come to the time when you could do it. I remember calling you back to tell you I loved you if I had forgotten to tell you during our just finished conversation. It was just something I needed to do.

Wednesday morning I called the doctor's office, first thing. First I spoke with the nurse, than with the doctor. They would have a morphine patch prescription ready in about an hour. You were really out of sorts this day. After I got you settled out in the porch, I left. You gave me directions, I knew the area, it was my old stomping grounds. Yeah, Bullshit. I missed his office by a couple of miles. But I found it. I found the drug store without incident. I approached the woman druggist, hoping perhaps she could fill this quickly and I could get home to you. She knew you. She did it right away. I met a lot of people like her throughout my journey with you. Most People were so kind. When I finally got home to you, you had a visitor. He was putting a larger air conditioner in the porch. I read faster than any Evelyn Wood graduate could on how the pain patch was to be applied. I put it on your arm. You stood up and said. "I know where I'm going". "What are you talking about". "I'm going with grama". "That's where I'm going to be buried." "What"!! I was dumbfounded. "My family and I decided where I'm going and it's with her." Only family I saw, was him and he never opened his mouth. I had no time or guts to think that far. I was more worried about this minute. You and I both know that you never wanted to go with Grama. You wanted to be with dad alone.

You were having trouble with your colostomy. You and I got you settled and comfortable in your chair. You watched TV, he finished what he was doing and I kept busy doing whatever I could to keep myself from falling apart. I wanted no part of the thought of burying you. I wanted you to stay with me. The patch was going to make it better. You would be feeling much better soon. At least that was what I had hoped for. Holy Jesus, did you get stoned. And boy was I jealous. You smiled the entire afternoon. Drank fluids when I asked you to and you were content even when the Spanish appeared on the closed caption. I went out early evening with my friend Agnes to get your special supplies. I was so torn about how much to buy. I could not believe that I was in a store buying your "stuff" with thoughts of life and death. I went the optimistic way and bought enough supplies to keep you going for at least a month. Agnes and I stopped for dinner on the way back and I called you from the restaurant. "You okay Betty Boop"? "I'm fine honey, Liz is here with me, don't worry." "Okey Dokey, Betty Boop" Agnes and I had some dinner and I ordered some side dishes to take home with me. It felt good to sit and have a beer with her. I spoke with her about what had taken place earlier in the morning. I also told Agnes about our conversation regarding who was going to make sure I was okay. Just in case. It took a long time for you to come to terms with my disability. You never really understood it until I came to take care of you. It was then that you saw, what my brain injury was all about. Just like you, I had good days and bad. I told you of my fears. If something happened to you, who was going to make sure I was okay. You told me you had asked your first born son to see to it that I was taken care of. He promised you that he would make sure I was all right. Either he lied to you mom or you lied to me.

Not that you would have lied to me on purpose mom. You would have done it just so I would feel like I had somewhere to go. You would have lied, only because it would be the only way, things could be the way you had hoped them to be. Who knew. Mom less than twenty four hours after you left, he threw me out of your house. Later on he changed the locks. In spite of him, I am all right. Sean and Helen made sure of that. And so do you, dad, and Gra. Thanks!

When I came home from dinner, Liz was gone and you were watching reruns of reruns of "Wings". It always amazed me how both you and daddy could watch the same rerun as many times as you did. The one time daddy didn't, I lost five bucks. I remember when you and dad came out to my "cottage". We were going to watch "Jeopardy". Daddy wanted to bet on the game. I said sure. I thought I was going to make an easy five bucks. I knew dad was more street smart than book smart. Somehow he won. I knew there was

not a chance in hell that he could have known
those answers. You never said a word. Turns out
he watched it at an earlier time before you left
your house. He did pretty good remembering the
answers. How did you ever get him to watch
Jeopardy anyhow? He watched "Archie" and
"Wings" so much so you would have thought he
must have known the dialogue by heart. I put the
packages down. And …..
     "Hey Betty Boop, What's up"? There you
went flying up off the chair. Scared the hell out of
me, cause I thought you heard me. You were by
now extremely stoned. You had the cutest smile
on your face. So peaceful like. You wanted to go to
bed. It was the first time we got you ready for bed
and you didn't ask for the aspirin. You went up
the stairs slowly. You seemed very tired. You
plopped on the bed. You were slow in helping me
get you ready but you sure were happy. You took
your book but your eyes were closed before your
head landed on the pillow. I kissed you on the

forehead and you opened your eyes, half way. "Goodnight honey" "Goodnight mom" I turned off the light. I stood out in the hall for a while. Then I sat on the top step for a while. You turned the light on. I waited to see what you were going to do. You opened your book. That lasted a minute and then you and the book were closed for the night. I turned off the light again, waited to see if you were settled and went down to the porch. I slept sitting up that night, never turning the TV off.

Morning seemed to come quickly this day. I had a cup of coffee and then went up to get you. You were sitting on the side of the bed. You were a little groggy, but when you had a wiseass remark to make about the coffee, I thought you were okay. "I'll be back in a few Betty Boop". "Okay honey". I went downstairs to give you a chance to have your coffee. I had another cup and went back up to get you. You didn't want to do anything. You even fought me on the shower thing but I won. You were pretty stoned. Somewhat like a gumby type of figure. We were moving slowly but we were getting things done. Going down the stairs scared me a bit. I would always go down ahead of you waiting at each step. Sometimes you even told me to get my big ass moving but today you stumbled twice. Your coordination was not good normally, today it bordered on what the hell is going on here? I had seen you tipsy in my day. This was not the same. This was whoa!!

We got you to your red chair in the porch and you plopped down in it. The way you landed even surprised you. "Mom, you want something to eat"? I was just asking for the hell of it. Your wobbly head looked at me funny and you didn't answer right away. You were looking like you had too much medicine or something. I wish I had known that this was the beginning of the end. "Mom I think I'm gonna take the patch off for a little while. Maybe it's a bit too much for you. Just for a little while." Before you could answer me I took the patch off. "What are you doing with my patch?" "Mom I just think it's a bit much for you right now". "We can put it back on later, as soon as you want it." "I think you're a little sensitive to this kind of stuff." I was going to try anything to fix this. I was dying inside. What was happening here? I was so trying not to panic. Your breathing was very shallow. Mine was like a freight train. "Mom are you all right"? "Yeah, I'm fine". This just didn't seem right to me. I know you had trouble hearing things but you had trouble understanding me. Your eyes looked really funny. "Mom, you want to eat something?" "Sure" "Whadda ya got?" Jesus she must be stoned, she hasn't eaten in three days. "I have mashed potatoes and creamed spinach that I brought home with me last night." "Wanna try some". I nuked you some spinach and potatoes as fast as I could. I thought if you could eat something you could come down from your high a little. While, I was trying to do things, I could feel my heart pounding in my chest and the echo of it in my ears. I gave you your plate and went and sat on the couch. You just sat there with the plate in your hand, and your arm resting on your knee. I watched you try to take a mouthful of food. You couldn't pick up the fork. "Mom. "You okay"?

You didn't answer me. "Mom". I got up and went over to you. I took the plate and fork from your hands. "Mom". You sat back in your chair. "Mom can you hear me". "Mom"? Your eyes were wide open and you had this glazed over, look about you. "Mom". Do you know who I am"? Mom'? . "Mom look at me, listen to me". "We have to get you over to the couch". "Come on honey pie we have to get up." "Hold on to me". "Come on mom, please." You looked at me and smiled. I got you standing and at the same time I tried to dial Sean on the phone. I got the recording and hung up. I threw the phone in the chair and tried to get you to walk. You couldn't. "Come on mom, just pick your foot up real slow, we have to get to the couch". "Mom you have to help me"? "Come on mom, please mom". I took my good hand and tapped you on the back of your leg and you picked it up. I did it again. Then you got going and we made it to the couch. You sat on the edge till I got the pillows ready for you and then I laid you down softly. You said you were cold so I covered you with the sheet. I pulled the rocking chair over and sat down. It was at that moment in time that you took my hands in yours and said these exact words. "It's coming to a beautiful head now honey". "I don't want you to worry." "It's going to be alright". "I love." You took my hands to your lips, and you kissed them. "Mom, I love you too". That was to be our last conversation. "Try and sleep mom". You already were. I called whom I was supposed to call. You went into a really deep sleep.

I sat there alone with you, rocking slowly.
When people started to come in, it got a little
hectic. I didn't want to share you with anyone.
Those who could be there were. We kept a vigil
throughout the day and night. I was going to sleep
on the living room couch. Kathy, Mike's wife told
me to go upstairs and sleep in your bed. I was
hesitant about sleeping in your bed. I was scared
to sleep in your bed. Kathy and I had spoken at
length about going to a better place and that this
was all a part of life. What Part? The part that
breaks your heart with seemingly little hope of it
ever feeling whole again. Is it the part where your
beliefs, take you to great comfort, in a mysterious
Eden? What is it? Little did I know, I would soon
have every page of my Faith tested. I went up to
your room. The darkness was shadowed by the
amber street lights from outside. The sounds that
had been a part of my childhood were busy
echoing throughout my weary mind. Your bed
looked so sad. It was so empty. Everyday, after

you were settled downstairs, I would come up here make the bed, check the height of the laundry pile and get things in order for the coming night. This morning past, I neglected your room. I am sorry. For weeks born before this night I would come up, turn down the bed and put the fan on high. I laid down on your bed cautiously, taking the pillow you used to hug yourself to sleep with and held it close, wiping my non negotiable tears on its soft white cotton cover. This day had been the longest of my life. This night would seem the shortest. My weary mind thought of all that went on that day. When Helen called from Dallas, she was so upset. She wanted to be here, she wanted to talk to you just once more. I told her to wait till she heard me say "Now" and then say what ever she wanted to say to you. I put the phone to your ear and said "now". I heard her plead for you to wait for her, that she was coming as fast as she could. That she loved you. To please wait for her. I know you heard her. I saw your hand, it made a

motion to try to hold the phone. Someone in the
back of me asked what I was doing. I ignored him.
Helen's was the last voice you heard on that
phone, you loved to hate. I'm glad you heard
Frank Sinatra too. It wasn't "My Way", but it was
Frank Sinatra's.

I had never felt such uncertainty in my life.
I must have slept. The hardest part of the day
seemed over, when my eyes had opened. Most
days, once I pass that, I figure I can handle just
about anything. It was early when I went down.
Most had gone and your first born and his nice
wife were getting ready to leave. They were going
home to shower and change but would be back
later on. "She could be like this for a while", was
what he said. I grabbed a cup of coffee and pulled
the rocking chair up to the couch. I put your
favorite morning program on the TV. Once again
you and I were alone again. I talked to you aloud.
I told you I loved you. I tried not to cry. Your
breathing changed. I called Sean. Sean came

immediately. Sat down in the rocker said good morning to you, looked at me and said. "Mom could be like this for a week or so". Some how I didn't think so. I was glad that Sean was here with you and I. I know he was with you when daddy died. He loves you guys so. He's so thankful to both you and dad for so many things. He's a good guy. We sat with you and talked as though you were in on the conversation. Sometimes in the silence I found myself drifting back in time. I could hear memories and see glimpses of you far from this place that was our present kismet. I found myself wanting to remember things long ago forgotten. I was trying so hard not to cry. I didn't. Since I spent most of my life saying I was sorry to you for one thing or another, I just wanted to thank you for things. There's so much, both good and bad, I am so very grateful to you for. The material things I know I thanked you for but there were things I never realized you had given me until I had to survive, life, myself…

🐚 Thank you for having me.

🐚 Thank you for coming to see me while I was incubating.

🐚 Thank you for naming me Mary Elizabeth.

🐚 Thank you for loving daddy when you could.

🐚 Thank you for the frilly white dress you made with the strawberries on the pockets. Sorry I played tackle football in it.

🐚 Thank you for "finger curls", hence my short hair. Mom it was the rags, they hurt like hell.

🐚 Thank you for my "Suzy Home Baker Oven" but you know now it didn't help.

🐚 Thank you for my first garter belt and the instructions on how to use it.

🐚 Thank you for not telling me about the birds and the bees. It kept me from coming home pregnant.

🐚 Thank you for all my brothers and sisters.

❧ Thank you for introducing me to grama.

❧ Thank you for classical music and Frank Sinatra, I found Elvis on my own.

❧ Thank you for defining unconditional love, nine different ways.

❧ Thank you for surviving so much despair, so that I could become the person I am.

❧ Thank you for not killing me when I thought Eau de Toilette from that little blue bottle, belonged in the toilet .

❧ Thank you for trying so hard, at everything life threw at you.

❧ Thank you for your wooden spoon, the sting of it instilled wisdom.

❧ Thank you for Jonathan Livingston Seagull.

❧ Thank you for Catholic School, the Sisters I am sure, feel otherwise.

🦋 Thank you for "The Catholic Girls Guide" 1963, I

still have it.

🦋 Thank you for understanding "my own thing" later

on, and letting me do it.

🦋 Thank you for laughing, making others wonder why.

🦋 Thank you for fresh baked bread, and Good Humor

Ice Cream while we sat on the curb.

🦋 Thank you for the stories about starving children in

other countries. I still eat everything on my plate,

and carry it everywhere, literally.

🦋 Thank you for not buying me everything I wanted

when I was little, I have little now, but what I have

means so much.

🐿 Thank you for reading me Paul Revere.

🐿 Thank you for not killing me, Lord knows,
sometimes you had ample reason to.

🐿
🐿 Thank you for not killing daddy.

🐿 Thank you for some of your denial, sometimes it can

be a positive.

🐿 Thank you for the rides on the roller coaster at

Nunely's.

🐿 Thank you for Mary Poppins, The Sound of Music,

and especially for Jesus Christ Superstar.

🐿 Thank you for not letting daddy kill me for the soda

bottle with the Liquor in it.

🐿 Thank you for trying so hard to make a lady out of

me, some of it worked.

🐿 Thank you for the "Plaid Stamps" on my birthday, I

will never forget my bow and arrow set .

🐿 Thank you for never giving up, at least not totally.

❧ Thank you for your thirst for reading. There wasn't much, that mystified you.

❧ Thank you for making Helen and I finish painting the house. That fifty dollar car was my first and the greatest.

❧ Thank you for class, I try.

❧ Thank you for staying to see me graduate with my Masters Degree, I could not have done it without you.

❧ Thank you for acknowledging, the person I have become, I know you didn't always understand, but you tried.

❧ Thank you for so few "I told you so".

❧ Thank you for leaving the way you did. Your appearance was angelic like…

I have never witnessed such peace in my life. You looked so beautiful mom, thru my aching tears, I watched as life ebbed from your physical being. Both Sean and I behaved as you would have wanted. We held both your hands and let you softly drift into eternal life. We were both pretty brave. Sean cupped your beautiful face in his hand and said "you go sweetheart, wherever it is you have to go". And your last breath, whispered goodbye. Through an undaunting silence, I felt something inside of me mom and I can't explain it. It was not fear nor sadness but something that I never felt before and it was okay . Something in me changed that day. That moment in time remains so precious in my soul that I know we will meet again, somewhere in painless

peace. You left so placidly, so graciously, so much the way you wanted.

🍀 Thank you for rowing your own boat, you never once dropped an oar.

🍀 Thank you, for your courage

🍀 Thank you for loving me,

God Bless.

May the road rise to meet you. May the wind be always at your back. May the sun shine warm upon your face, the rains fall soft upon your fields and until we meet again, may God hold you in the palm of His hand .

an Irish blessing

Love

Mary

My experience with my mother gave me the strength to go through the technical things that occur from death. In our Irish Catholic fishbowl, we had the family fight, the wake, the family fight, the burial, and finally the family no longer on speaking terms. It also gave me the strength to let her go. I did everything within my own ability to make it okay for her. It was the least I could do for the woman who bore me, raised me and forgave me. I could ask for no greater gift than the one I carry with me, I learned to never give up hope. Even in the darkest hours, Faith holds the light. Once you open your eyes, the rest is cake.

Opening my eyes was the most demanding obstacle I came across while I was with my mother. I'm not sure if she ever really accepted the fact that she was dying. Sometimes I thought she did and others times not. My accepting it, looking at what was happening right here now, was the most difficult fragment of my journey with my mother. Like her, sometimes I did look at reality and sometimes I didn't. Those times it was just to painful. For a long time after she left I thought I killed her. This was not an Irish guilt thing but that I had really done her in, when I got the patch for her. A friend was kind enough to tell me that she was ready to go, the patch just helped her relax enough to let go. I wouldn't trade a lifetime, for what I had with my mother that year. I wish the others could have seen the woman she had become. What she did for herself was best. What she did for me was awesome.

ELIZABETH - CIRCA 1947

ISBN 141202218-5